AF482038

HOME OFFICE HERO

HOME OFFICE HERO

Secrets to Skyrocketing Productivity from Your Living Room

B. VINCENT

QuantumQuill Press

Contents

Copyright @ 2024 by B. Vincent

All rights reserved. No part of this book may be reproduced in any manner whatsoever without written permission except in the case of brief quotations embodied in critical articles and reviews.

First Printing, 2024

I

Chapter 1: The Power of Working from Home

Prologue to Remote Work Upset

Lately, a critical change in outlook has happened in the domain of business, with the conventional office-based model giving way to the ascent of remote work. This part sets out on an excursion to investigate the key changes and uncommon open doors achieved by this remote work upheaval.

As we dig into the scene of remote work, we experience a plenty of insights and studies that highlight its outstanding development and unquestionable effect. From new businesses to Fortune 500 organizations, associations of all sizes are embracing remote work as a practical and profitable choice for their labor force. The adaptability and opportunity managed the cost of by remote work are reshaping the manner in which we see and move toward business, prompting a change in the actual texture of the cutting edge working environment.

Besides, remote work isn't simply a pattern; it's a development energized by substantial advantages and genuine outcomes. For representatives, the appeal of adaptable timetables, decreased drive times, and further developed balance between serious and fun activities is picture, showing that telecommuters frequently display more elevated levels of efficiency and occupation fulfillment. With the adaptability to structure their working day around top efficiency hours and individual responsibilities, telecommuters are enabled to convey results according to their own preferences.

Another normal confusion is the conviction that remote work obstructs correspondence and joint effort. Pundits contend that without eye to eye collaboration, groups might battle to convey really and cultivate a feeling of brotherhood. However, headways in innovation have made it more straightforward than at any other time for remote groups to remain associated and team up consistently. From video conferencing devices to project the executives stages, a plenty of computerized arrangements exist to overcome any barrier and work with compelling correspondence in remote work settings.

Besides, there's a misinterpretation that remote work is inseparable from disconnection and depression. Pundits contend that without the social connection of a customary office, telecommuters might feel separated and confined. Notwithstanding, remote work offers open doors for significant associations and local area building, whether through virtual group gatherings, online discussions, or collaborating spaces. By effectively searching out open doors for association and cooperation, telecommuters can develop a feeling of having a place and fellowship, even from a far distance.

Fundamentally, this part fills in as a clarion call to challenge the misinterpretations that frequently encompass remote work. By going up against these fantasies head-on, we engage ourselves to embrace the conceivable outcomes and amazing open doors that remote work bears. As we proceed with our excursion into the universe of remote work, let us cast to the side confusions and embrace the real factors of this extraordinary approach to working with receptive outlooks and open hearts.

Turning into a Useful Work space Legend

As we set out on our investigation of remote work, it's fundamental to develop the mentality of a work space legend — a proactive and enabled way to deal with exploring the difficulties and chances of telecommuting. This part fills in as an energizing weep for people to embrace their true capacity and adapt to the situation as heroes of efficiency and progress in the work space climate.

To turn into a useful work space legend, one must initially perceive the remarkable open doors and difficulties inborn in remote work. By recognizing the opportunity and adaptability managed the cost of by remote work, people can bridle these characteristics to upgrade their balance between fun and serious activities and efficiency. Additionally, by defying normal traps and snags head-on, work space legends can foster strength and versatility notwithstanding misfortune.

Key to the ethos of the work space legend is a promise to proactive self-administration and responsibility. By taking responsibility for time and assignments, work space legends can focus on actually and remain on track in the midst of interruptions. Whether through time-impeding procedures, objective setting systems, or efficiency devices, work space legends engage themselves to amplify their proficiency and result in the work space climate.

Moreover, work space legends comprehend the significance of keeping up with limits and taking care of oneself in their remote work venture. By laying out clear limits among work and individual life, people can forestall burnout and save their prosperity. Also, by focusing on taking care of oneself practices like activity, care, and breaks all through the average working day, work space legends support their energy and concentration for the long stretch.

Basically, this part fills in as a source of inspiration for people to embrace the mantle of the work space legend and open their maximum capacity in the remote work scene. By taking on a proactive and engaged outlook, people can explore the intricacies of remote work with certainty and beauty, arising as guides of efficiency and outcome in their work space conditions. As we proceed with our excursion into the universe of remote work, let us regard the call to become work space legends, ready to vanquish difficulties and jump all over chances on the way to proficient satisfaction and self-awareness.

2

Chapter 2: Crafting Your Ideal Home Office Space

Surveying Your Requirements and Inclinations

Setting out on the excursion of creating your ideal work space starts with a vital stage: figuring out your special necessities and inclinations. In this part, we dig into the complexities of self-evaluation, enabling you to recognize the fundamental components that will add to your efficiency and solace in your home work area.

Prior to jumping into the actual parts of your work space arrangement, pause for a minute to consider your singular prerequisites. Consider factors, for example, your work style, work liabilities, and individual inclinations. Might it be said that you are somebody who flourishes in a moderate climate, or do you favor a space loaded up with energetic varieties and rousing style? Do you require adequate normal light to remain stimulated and centered, or do you favor a comfortable niche concealed from interruptions?

Then, survey the reasonable contemplations that will shape your work space plan. Check out any ergonomic necessities, like appropriate seating and work area level, to help your stance and forestall inconvenience. Consider the spatial requirements of your home and how you

6

can amplify the accessible region to make a productive and utilitarian work area. Furthermore, contemplate the gear and devices you'll have to play out your occupation really, from a solid web association with fundamental peripherals like printers and scanners.

By finding opportunity to assess your necessities and inclinations, you establish the groundwork for a work space that is custom fitted to your exceptional prerequisites. Furnished with this mindfulness, you can certainly push ahead in planning a work area that meets your pragmatic requirements as well as mirrors your character and upgrades your general prosperity. As we proceed with our investigation of making the ideal work space, let us embrace the course of self-disclosure and plan with energy and reason.

Planning an Ergonomic and Agreeable Arrangement

Whenever you've surveyed your requirements and inclinations, the following stage in creating your ideal work space is to zero in on planning a climate that focuses on solace and ergonomics. In this section, we dive into the standards of ergonomic plan and proposition useful ways to make a work area that upholds your actual prosperity while improving efficiency.

Ergonomics, the study of planning items and conditions to expand human prosperity and execution, assumes a basic part in the work space setting. By adjusting your work area to ergonomic standards, you can limit the gamble of uneasiness and injury related with delayed times of sitting and working at a PC.

Start by choosing furniture that advances appropriate stance and arrangement. Put resources into an agreeable and steady seat that offers satisfactory lumbar help and considers simple change of seat level and slant. Your work area ought to be at a level that permits your arms to rest serenely at a 90-degree point while composing, with adequate room to oblige your PC screen, console, and other fundamental frill.

Consider the format of your work area and how it works with development and work process. Organize your work area and seat in a manner that considers simple admittance to oftentimes utilized things, limiting the requirement for coming to or stressing. Keep links and

cations and programming arrangements accessible to advance your work process and upgrade your productivity. From project the executives stages like Trello and Asana to specialized devices like Leeway and Microsoft Groups, there's an abundance of choices to suit each need and inclination.

Exploit distributed storage administrations to safely store and access your records from anyplace, taking out the requirement for actual capacity gadgets and guaranteeing consistent joint effort with far off partners. Administrations like Google Drive, Dropbox, and OneDrive proposition hearty elements for record sharing, synchronizing, and variant control, permitting you to remain coordinated and useful without the problem of overseeing actual documents.

Moreover, consider coordinating computerization instruments and work processes into your work space arrangement to smooth out redundant errands and amplify proficiency. From email channels and planning collaborators to work process mechanization stages like Zapier and IFTTT, computerization offers a strong method for limiting physical work and save time for more significant work.

By utilizing innovation and advanced devices in your work space arrangement, you can open new degrees of efficiency and effectiveness, engaging you to accomplish your objectives and succeed in your work. As we proceed with our investigation of creating the ideal work space, let us embrace the extraordinary capability of innovation to improve our efficiency and lift our expert abilities.

3

Chapter 3: Mastering Time Management Techniques

Grasping the Significance of Using time productively

In the domain of remote work, where the limits among expert and individual life can obscure, excelling at using time effectively becomes an expertise as well as a need for progress. This section fills in as a fundamental investigation into the basic job that compelling time usage plays in streamlining efficiency, decreasing pressure, and cultivating a solid balance between serious and fun activities in a remote work setting.

At the core of compelling time usage lies the acknowledgment of time as a limited and valuable asset. In reality as we know it where interruptions flourish and requests continually compete for our focus, the capacity to allot time shrewdly and deliberately becomes vital. By understanding the worth of every second and focusing on assignments likewise, telecommuters can augment their efficiency and achieve more quicker than expected.

Besides, viable time usage fills in as a strong remedy to the unavoidable pressure and overpower that can go with remote work. By laying out clear objectives, setting sensible cutoff times, and separating errands into reasonable pieces, people can explore their responsibility with certainty and lucidity. Instead of feeling overpowered by the sheer volume of undertakings, telecommuters can move toward their normal working day with a feeling of direction and control, prompting expanded fulfillment and prosperity.

Besides, using time effectively reaches out past the domain of expert obligations to incorporate all parts of life. By dealing with our time successfully, we make space for function as well as for special goals, connections, and taking care of oneself. By finding some kind of harmony among work and individual life, telecommuters can forestall burnout, sustain their prosperity, and lead satisfying lives both on and off the clock.

Basically, this part fills in as a clarion call to perceive and focus on the significance of time usage with regards to remote work. As we proceed with our investigation of dominating time usage procedures, let us embrace the force of deliberateness and reason in molding our days, recovering control within recent memory, and opening our maximum capacity in the remote work scene.

Carrying out Time-Impeding Systems

Time-hindering stands as a signal of construction and association in the midst of the ocean of undertakings and obligations that characterize the remote work scene. In this part, we dive into the specialty of time-hindering — a strong procedure for focusing on undertakings, overseeing time successfully, and streamlining efficiency in the work space climate.

At its center, time-hindering spins around the idea of designating explicit blocks of time to individual undertakings or exercises over the course of the day. By devoting engaged, continuous periods to high-need errands, telecommuters can limit interruptions and amplify their effectiveness. Besides, time-impeding offers a feeling of construction and beat to the working day, assisting people with keeping up with force and remain focused towards their objectives.

To execute time-impeding successfully, start by distinguishing your most significant assignments and responsibilities for the afternoon or week ahead. Focus on undertakings in view of direness, significance, and cutoff time, dispensing committed blocks of time to handle each errand with centered consideration and purposefulness.

Then, lay out a reliable daily schedule for your time-obstructing work on, cutting out assigned blocks of time for various kinds of exercises or undertakings. Whether it's distributing a block of opportunity in the first part of the day for profound work, planning more limited blocks for email the board and regulatory undertakings, or making opportunity for breaks and unwinding, make a system that lines up with your normal rhythms and inclinations.

As you execute time-impeding into your day to day daily practice, stay adaptable and versatile to the inescapable moves and changes that emerge over the course of the day. While it's fundamental to stick to your arranged timetable however much as could reasonably be expected, permit yourself the adaptability to change and redistribute time blocks on a case by case basis in light of startling occasions or arising needs.

Besides, influence advanced apparatuses and assets to help your time-obstructing practice, whether it's utilizing schedule applications to plan and picture your time blocks or errand the board devices to follow progress and remain coordinated. Try different things with various methods and procedures to find the methodology that turns out best for you, refining and adjusting your time-hindering practice over the long run to suit your advancing necessities and conditions.

Basically, time-hindering fills in as a foundation of successful using time productively, giving an organized system to expanding efficiency and accomplishing balance in the remote workplace. As we proceed with our excursion of dominating time usage procedures, let us embrace the force of time-obstructing to open our maximum capacity and flourish in the steadily changing scene of remote work.

Procedures for Combatting Stalling

Tarrying, the lasting adversary of efficiency, hides in the shadows of each and every telecommuter's excursion. In this section, we face this imposing foe head-on, investigating methods and methodologies to conquer tarrying and recover control within recent memory and concentration in the work space climate.

As we explore the sensitive dance of balance between fun and serious activities in the remote work scene, let us focus on the foundation and support of clear limits. By protecting our own time and prosperity, we can develop versatility, forestall burnout, and lead satisfying lives both inside and beyond work.

4

Chapter 4: Developing Healthy Habits for Remote Success

Laying out an Everyday Daily practice

In the liquid and frequently flighty universe of remote work, the foundation of a reliable everyday schedule arises as a guide of dependability and construction. This section digs into the significance of organizing your day purposefully to streamline efficiency, encourage center, and advance by and large prosperity in the remote workplace.

A very much created everyday schedule fills in as a guide for exploring the intricacies of remote work, giving a structure to overseeing time really and accomplishing objectives productively. By laying out a set timetable for your working day, you can limit interruptions, decrease choice weakness, and make an ability to keep in tempo and consistency in your day to day routine.

Start by defining clear limits around your work hours, assigning explicit times for beginning and finishing work every day. Impart your accessibility to partners and clients, guaranteeing that others regard your assigned work hours and comprehend when you are inaccessible for gatherings or interferences.

Then, structure your day to oblige the different assignments and obligations that involve your work and individual life. Dispense time blocks for various kinds of exercises, like centered work, gatherings, breaks, and individual undertakings, guaranteeing a reasonable circulation of significant investment over the course of the day.

Integrate ceremonies and propensities into your day to day everyday practice to flag changes between various exercises and develop a feeling of consistency and consistency. Whether it's beginning your day with a morning standard, enjoying normal reprieves to re-energize and pull together, or slowing down with a loosening up night custom, ceremonies give anchor focuses that ground you in the midst of the rhythmic movement of day to day existence.

In addition, be aware of the significance of adaptability and flexibility in your everyday daily practice, perceiving that unexpected occasions and disturbances might require changes en route. Embrace the soul of trial and error and emphasis, refining your everyday practice over the long haul to more readily line up with your advancing requirements and conditions.

As we set out on the excursion of laying out a day to day daily practice for far off progress, let us embrace the force of design and deliberateness to open our maximum capacity and flourish in the unique scene of remote work. By creating an everyday schedule that fills in as an establishment for efficiency, prosperity, and satisfaction, we can explore the difficulties and chances of remote work with certainty and effortlessness.

Integrating Activity into Your Day

In the midst of the requests of remote work, the significance of actual work for keeping up with generally speaking wellbeing and prosperity couldn't possibly be more significant. In this part, we investigate the advantages of coordinating activity into your day to day daily schedule and proposition viable systems for integrating development into your average working day, even inside the bounds of your home.

Actual work fills in as a strong counteractant to the stationary idea of numerous remote workplaces, offering a heap of advantages for both body and brain. From working on cardiovascular wellbeing and helping safe capability to lessening pressure and improving temperament, normal activity assumes a critical part in supporting ideal physical and mental prosperity in the remote work scene.

Start by saving devoted time for practice in your day to day daily schedule, focusing on development as a fundamental part of your taking care of oneself routine. Whether it's cutting out time for a morning exercise, going for a noontime stroll break, or consolidating short development breaks over the course of the day, track down potential chances to imbue your day with actual work.

Investigate an assortment of activity modalities to find what turns out best for yourself and lines up with your inclinations and wellness objectives. Whether it's high-impact exercises like strolling, running, or cycling, strength preparing practices utilizing bodyweight or obstruction groups, or psyche body practices like yoga or jujitsu, pick exercises that you appreciate and that give you pleasure and essentialness.

Embrace the adaptability and innovativeness managed the cost of by remote work to incorporate development flawlessly into your day, even inside the bounds of your home or work area. Think about setting up an assigned exercise region in your home, outfitted with gym equipment or wellness frill, to work with helpful and open exercises over the course of the day.

Additionally, influence innovation and advanced assets to help your wellness process, whether it's tracking with online exercise recordings, keeping tabs on your development with wellness applications, or interfacing with virtual wellness networks for help and responsibility.

As we set out on the excursion of integrating exercise into our everyday daily practice for far off progress, let us focus on our actual wellbeing and prosperity as fundamental mainstays of efficiency and satisfaction. By embracing development as a foundation of our taking care of oneself routine, we can develop versatility, essentialness, and do. Whether it's eating carefully, relishing each nibble and valuing the sustenance it gives, or taking part in careful correspondence, listening profoundly and answering with sympathy and empathy, care offers a pathway to more noteworthy association and satisfaction in our regular routines.

Notwithstanding care, focus on taking care of oneself exercises that support your body, brain, and soul, recharging your stores and advancing in general prosperity. Whether taking part in leisure activities and interests give you pleasure and satisfaction, investing energy in nature, or rehearsing demonstrations of self-empathy and generosity, taking care of oneself is fundamental for keeping up with strength and forestalling burnout in the remote work scene.

As we explore the dynamic and frequently requesting scene of remote work, let us focus on our psychological and close to home prosperity as fundamental mainstays of our prosperity and satisfaction. By embracing care and taking care of oneself practices with purposefulness and sympathy, we can develop flexibility, imperativeness, and bliss in the remote work scene, permitting us to flourish both actually and expertly.

5

Chapter 5: Communication and Collaboration in the Virtual Workspace

The Significance of Successful Correspondence

In the virtual work area, where actual distance isolates colleagues and correspondence happens basically through advanced channels, the significance of compelling correspondence couldn't possibly be more significant. This part fills in as a profound jump into the basic job that correspondence plays in remote workplaces, featuring its ability to encourage cooperation, arrangement, and group union across geological limits.

At the core of compelling correspondence lies the capacity to pass on thoughts, data, and assumptions plainly and compactly, guaranteeing that all colleagues are in total agreement and pursuing shared objectives. Without any up close and personal association, remote groups depend intensely on composed and verbal correspondence through email, visit, video calls, and other advanced stages to facilitate errands, trade input, and simply decide.

Successful correspondence works with the smooth progression of data as well as develops a feeling of association and having a place among colleagues. By cultivating open and straightforward correspondence channels, remote groups can construct trust, empower joint effort, and establish a strong and comprehensive workplace where everybody feels esteemed and heard.

Besides, powerful correspondence fills in as a key part for fruitful venture the executives and execution in the remote work scene. Clear correspondence of assumptions, cutoff times, and expectations assists with forestalling errors and alleviate chances, guaranteeing that undertakings keep focused and meet their goals.

As we explore the virtual work area, let us focus on the development of compelling relational abilities as fundamental apparatuses for progress. By embracing clearness, straightforwardness, and sympathy in our correspondence rehearses, we can overcome any issues of actual distance and assemble solid and tough groups fit for accomplishing remarkable outcomes in the remote workplace.

Utilizing Computerized Devices for Cooperation

In the steadily developing scene of remote work, computerized apparatuses arise as significant partners chasing consistent correspondence and joint effort. This part dives into the assorted cluster of advanced stages and devices accessible to remote groups, offering bits of knowledge and procedures for choosing and utilizing these apparatuses successfully to work with joint effort and upgrade efficiency.

The computerized tool compartment accessible to remote groups is immense and fluctuated, including a large number of stages and applications intended to smooth out correspondence, project the executives, record sharing, and that's only the tip of the iceberg. From informing applications like Leeway and Microsoft Groups to project the board devices like Asana and Trello, the choices are for all intents and purposes boundless, permitting groups to tailor their tool stash to suit their extraordinary requirements and inclinations.

While choosing advanced apparatuses for cooperation, it's fundamental to consider factors like convenience, versatility, combination capacities, and security highlights. Pick devices that line up with your group's work process and correspondence style, guaranteeing that they improve productivity and viability as opposed to adding pointless intricacy or grating to your cycles.

Besides, embrace the force of reconciliation to make a consistent and interconnected computerized environment that upholds cooperation across different stages and applications. Search for devices that offer vigorous reconciliation abilities, permitting you to adjust information and work processes between various frameworks and smooth out cross-practical joint effort.

Whenever you've chosen your computerized tool stash, put time and assets into onboarding and preparing to guarantee that colleagues are capable in utilizing these apparatuses successfully. Offer continuous help and direction to address any difficulties or obstructions that emerge, enabling colleagues to use advanced devices to their fullest potential.

As we bridle the force of computerized devices for coordinated effort in the virtual work area, let us embrace development and flexibility as we explore the steadily changing scene of remote work. By utilizing innovation to cultivate correspondence, coordination, and joint effort, remote groups can rise above geological limits and accomplish momentous outcomes in quest for their common objectives and goals.

Exploring Virtual Gatherings and Video Meetings

In the virtual scene of remote work, gatherings and video meetings act as fundamental discussions for cooperation, direction, and relationship-building. This section dives into the subtleties of leading useful and connecting with virtual gatherings, offering methodologies and strategies for boosting cooperation, cultivating association, and keeping up with center in advanced settings.

Virtual gatherings present novel difficulties and open doors contrasted with their in-person partners. Without the advantage of actual presence, remote groups should depend on computerized stages and specialized devices to work with significant connection and correspondence. All things considered, moving toward virtual gatherings with

6

Chapter 6: Navigating Distractions and Staying Focused

Distinguishing Normal Interruptions in the Remote Workplace

In the powerful scene of remote work, interruptions hide everywhere, prepared to seize our concentration and wreck our efficiency. This section leaves on an excursion to distinguish the heap interruptions that plague remote workplaces, revealing insight into their deceptive nature and investigating their unfavorable consequences for our capacity to focus and perform.

Remote work presents an extraordinary arrangement of interruptions that contrast from those experienced in customary office settings. From the charm of family tasks and individual tasks to the alarm call of virtual entertainment and advanced notices, the impulses to wander from our work obligations are ever-present, taking steps to disturb our work process and subvert our efficiency.

Perceiving and understanding the effect of interruptions is the most important move towards recovering our concentration and efficiency in the remote workplace. By focusing a light on normal interruptions, for example, email over-burden, performing various tasks, and surrounding commotion, we can foster more noteworthy consciousness of the snags that substitute our direction and devise procedures to defeat them.

In addition, it's fundamental to recognize the mental and close to home cost that interruptions can take on our prosperity. Continually moving our consideration starting with one assignment then onto the next can prompt expanded pressure, weariness, and mental over-burden, making it hard to support center and accomplish our objectives over the long haul.

As we explore the labyrinth of interruptions in the remote work scene, let us arm ourselves with mindfulness and purposefulness to defeat these impediments and recover our concentration. By recognizing normal interruptions and understanding their effect, we can find proactive ways to limit their impact and establish a favorable workplace that encourages efficiency, inventiveness, and prosperity.

Techniques for Limiting Interruptions and Keeping up with Concentration

In the never-ending fight against interruptions, furnished with the munititions stockpile of mindfulness, now is the ideal time to dive into significant procedures to brace our concentration and efficiency in the remote workplace. This part fills in as a manual, offering a plenty of reasonable methods and strategies to battle interruptions and develop an extremely careful concentration on our main jobs.

One of the most intense methodologies for limiting interruptions is to establish a favorable workplace that upholds fixation and concentration. Assign a committed work area liberated from mess and interruptions, where you can submerge yourself in your work without outer interferences. Lay out limits with family individuals or flat mates, conveying the significance of continuous work time and enrolling their help in limiting interruptions.

Then, influence innovation for your potential benefit by using efficiency devices and applications intended to assist you with remaining on track and coordinated. From time-following applications that screen your efficiency to program expansions that block diverting sites and web-based entertainment, innovation offers an abundance of assets to keep interruptions under control and keep up with your emphasis on the job needing to be done.

Practice the craft of using time effectively and prioritization to designate your significant investment astutely, zeroing in on high-need errands and limiting time spent on low-esteem exercises. Break your average business day into centered blocks of time devoted to explicit assignments, limiting performing various tasks and boosting efficiency. Use procedures like the Pomodoro Method, which includes working to put it plainly, engaged blasts followed by brief breaks, to keep up with energy and forestall burnout.

Also, be proactive in defining limits and overseeing interruptions that emerge over the course of the day. Quietness warnings on your gadgets, set explicit times for browsing email and answering messages, and lay out customs and schedules to flag advances among work and rest. By assuming command over your current circumstance and carrying out these methodologies reliably, you can establish a climate helpful for profound work and supported center in the remote work scene.

As we set out on the excursion of limiting interruptions and keeping up with center, let us embrace the force of purposefulness and train to defeat the impediments that substitute our direction. By executing these systems with steadiness and constancy, we can recover our concentration, help our efficiency, and accomplish our objectives with clearness and reason in the remote workplace.

Rehearsing Care and Consideration The executives

In the clamor of interruptions that characterize the remote workplace, the act of care arises as a signal of clearness and concentration in the midst of the bedlam. This section digs into the groundbreaking force of care and consideration the executives strategies, offering a pathway to develop elevated mindfulness and focus despite interruptions.

At its center, care includes the development of present-second mindfulness and non-critical acknowledgment of our viewpoints, feelings, and environmental elements. By focusing on careful our encounters, we can develop a feeling of lucidity and presence that permits us to explore interruptions effortlessly and versatility.

Start by integrating care rehearses into your everyday daily practice, saving devoted time for reflection, profound breathing activities, or body outputs to ground yourself right now and calm the perpetual prattle of the psyche. Use care as a device to moor yourself in the midst of the twirl of interruptions, permitting you to keep up with spotlight and lucidity on your jobs that needs to be done.

Besides, practice consideration the board strategies to prepare your brain to keep on track and mindful despite interruptions. Explore different avenues regarding strategies like single-entrusting, where you give your undivided focus to each assignment in turn, or attentional pulling together, where you delicately divert your concentration back to the job needing to be done at whatever point your brain meanders.

Integrate care into your average business day by rehearsing careful work methods, like careful eating or careful strolling, to implant snapshots of care into your day to day exercises. Use care as a focal point through which to move toward your work, developing a feeling of interest and receptiveness that permits you to connect all the more completely with your errands and partners.

As we set out on the excursion of rehearsing care and consideration the executives in the remote work scene, let us embrace the force of presence and attention to conquer interruptions and recover our concentration. By developing care as a day to day practice, we can explore the difficulties of remote work with lucidity, versatility, and effortlessness, permitting us to accomplish our objectives no sweat and satisfaction.

Building Versatility and Flexibility Despite Interruptions

In the unusual territory of remote work, interruptions are an unavoidable piece of the scene. In any case, it's not just about limiting interruptions; it's additionally about building versatility and flexibility to really explore them. This section dives into the significance of developing strength and flexibility as fundamental abilities for keeping up with concentration and efficiency despite interruptions.

for our prosperity and efficiency is the most important move towards conquering the difficulties of detachment in the remote work scene. Individuals are intrinsically friendly animals, wired for association and having a place, and the shortfall of significant social cooperations can have significant ramifications for our psychological and close to home wellbeing.

Besides, detachment in remote workplaces can worsen existing sensations of an inability to embrace success and self-question, enhancing our internal pundit and sabotaging our trust in our capacities. Without the help and approval of our friends and partners, we might battle to keep an identity worth and capability in our work.

As we explore the intricacies of seclusion in the remote work scene, let us recognize the significant effect it can have on our prosperity and efficiency. By understanding the foundations of separation and its impacts on our psychological and profound wellbeing, we can start to find proactive ways to defeat sensations of depression and disengagement and develop a feeling of having a place and local area in the virtual work area.

Techniques for Beating Sensations of Segregation

As we go up against the unavoidable test of detachment in remote workplaces, it becomes basic to outfit ourselves with powerful systems for battling dejection and cultivating association. This part fills in as an encouraging sign, offering reasonable methods and strategies to explore the cloudy waters of seclusion and develop significant associations in the virtual domain.

One of the most powerful techniques for conquering sensations of detachment is to focus on ordinary and deliberate social associations with partners and companions. Plan virtual quick rests, lunch gatherings, or casual catch-ups with partners to cultivate a feeling of kinship and association. Use video conferencing stages to participate in up close and personal discussions while conceivable, permitting you to peruse looks and non-verbal communication and fortify your social securities.

Additionally, influence computerized devices and stages to make virtual networks and encouraging groups of people where telecommuters can associate, team up, and share encounters. Whether it's through web-based gatherings, online entertainment gatherings, or virtual interest-based clubs, track down chances to draw in with similar people who share your inclinations and values.

Search out mentorship and backing from additional accomplished associates or friends who can offer direction, guidance, and consolation in exploring the difficulties of remote work. Lay out normal registrations or mentorship meetings to associate with guides and mentees, cultivating a feeling of responsibility and shared help in accomplishing your expert objectives.

In conclusion, focus on taking care of oneself and prosperity as fundamental parts of beating sensations of confinement in the remote work scene. Enjoy reprieves when required, take part in exercises that give you pleasure and satisfaction, and focus on your psychological and close to home wellbeing as you explore the intricacies of remote work.

As we explore the excursion of conquering segregation and developing association in the remote work scene, let us embrace the force of deliberateness and local area to fashion significant connections and encourage a feeling of having a place in the virtual work area. By executing these systems with constancy and persistence, we can defeat the difficulties of confinement and flourish in the interconnected universe of remote work.

Sustaining Significant Connections in the Remote Work Scene

In the advanced field of remote work, where up close and personal connections are scant, supporting significant associations with partners and companions becomes principal. This section digs into the specialty of encouraging credible associations and developing brotherhood in virtual work settings, offering bits of knowledge and methods to assemble trust, affinity, and local area in the remote work scene.

At the core of sustaining significant connections in the remote work scene lies the development of legitimacy and weakness in our collaborations. Share your encounters, difficulties, and victories transparently with your partners, cultivating a culture of straightforwardness and trust that establishes the groundwork for significant associations and joint effort.

Put time and exertion into getting to know your partners on an individual level, past their expert jobs and obligations. Participate in virtual group building exercises, icebreaker games, or casual talks to separate hindrances and cultivate a feeling of fellowship and having a place inside the group.

In addition, focus on undivided attention and compassion in your connections with associates, trying to figure out their viewpoints, sentiments, and necessities. Practice sympathy by imagining their perspective and answering with empathy and figuring out, even in snapshots of conflict or struggle.

Influence advanced stages and specialized devices to work with association and coordinated effort with far off partners, whether it's through video calls, texting, or virtual cooperation spaces. Use innovation as an extension to beat actual distance and encourage significant associations with partners no matter what their area.

As we explore the remote work scene, let us embrace the valuable chance to develop significant connections and encourage a feeling of local area in the computerized domain. By sustaining validness, compassion, and association in our cooperations with partners, we can major areas of strength for assemble tough groups fit for accomplishing phenomenal outcomes in quest for our common objectives and desires.

Utilizing Innovation to Work with Association and Cooperation

In the computerized time of remote work, innovation fills in as a useful asset for overcoming any barrier of actual distance and encouraging association and coordinated effort among remote groups. This part investigates the urgent job of innovation in working with significant associations and improving cooperation in virtual workplaces, offering bits of knowledge and methodologies to use advanced stages and specialized apparatuses actually.

Embrace the horde of computerized stages and specialized devices accessible to remote groups, utilizing them to make virtual spaces where partners can interface, team up, and convey flawlessly. From video conferencing stages like Zoom and Microsoft Groups to coordinated effort instruments like Leeway and Asana, pick devices that line up with your group's work process and correspondence inclinations, guaranteeing that they improve proficiency and adequacy as opposed to adding pointless intricacy to your cycles.

Influence video conferencing innovation to lead virtual gatherings, meetings to generate new ideas, and group building exercises that cultivate association and joint effort among remote colleagues. Use video calls to participate in eye to eye discussions, permitting you to peruse looks and non-verbal communication and fortify social securities with associates no matter what their actual area.

Also, investigate the capability of virtual joint effort spaces and task the board apparatuses to work with collaboration and coordination among remote groups. Make shared reports, schedules, and undertaking records to keep everybody adjusted and on target, encouraging a feeling of responsibility and straightforwardness in your cooperative endeavors.

Tackle the force of computerized specialized instruments, for example, texting and email to work with ongoing correspondence and data dividing between remote colleagues. Utilize these devices to give refreshes, share assets, and seek clarification on pressing issues, encouraging a culture of open correspondence and joint effort in the virtual work area.

As we explore the computerized scene of remote work, let us embrace the extraordinary force of innovation to work with association and joint effort among remote groups. By utilizing advanced stages and specialized apparatuses actually, we can beat the hindrances of actual distance and cultivate significant associations that drive development, imagination, and progress in the remote workplace.

In addition, practice self-sympathy and flexibility even with mishaps and difficulties. Perceive that disappointment isn't an impression of our value or capacities yet a chance for learning and development. Develop a feeling of flexibility by quickly returning from mishaps with beauty and assurance, realizing that each challenge we defeat reinforces our strength and invigorates our determination.

Put forth objectives that stretch and challenge you, pushing you outside your usual range of familiarity and touching off your energy for learning and development. Separate your objectives into reasonable advances and celebrate progress en route, recognizing your accomplishments and achievements as you forge ahead with your excursion of individual and expert turn of events.

As we explore the intricacies of remote work, let us embrace the groundbreaking force of a development outlook to explore change, defeat difficulties, and open our maximum capacity. By developing versatility, self-sympathy, and an enthusiasm for learning, we can set out on an excursion of nonstop development and expert improvement that enhances our lives and impels us towards progress.

Utilizing On the web Assets and Learning Stages

In the advanced period of remote work, an overflow of online assets and learning stages stands prepared to fuel our excursion of nonstop learning and expert turn of events. This section dives into the tremendous scene of web based learning potential open doors, offering experiences and systems to tackle the force of computerized schooling to improve our abilities, information, and capacities in the remote workplace.

Investigate the huge swath of online courses, online classes, and instructive materials accessible on stages like Coursera, Udemy, and LinkedIn Learning, among others. From specialized abilities like coding and information examination to delicate abilities like correspondence and initiative, these stages offer a mother lode of courses taking care of a great many interests and learning targets.

Influence the adaptability and availability of internet figuring out how to fit your expert advancement excursion to your exceptional requirements and inclinations. Pick courses and materials that line up with your vocation objectives, interests, and learning style, permitting you to redo your opportunity for growth and boost its effect on your own and proficient development.

Additionally, embrace the force of independent figuring out how to take responsibility for proficient improvement venture. Put away devoted time for learning and development, laying out a daily practice and construction that upholds your continuous training and expertise improvement. Utilize web based learning stages to enhance and improve your current information and skill, filling holes and extending your viewpoints in areas of interest or need.

Draw in with online networks and discussions to associate with similar people and grow your organization of friends and guides. Partake in conversations, share bits of knowledge and encounters, and team up on activities or drives to improve your opportunity for growth and encourage significant associations in the computerized domain.

As we explore the computerized scene of remote work, let us embrace the extraordinary force of internet figuring out how to improve our abilities, expand our perspectives, and drive our vocations forward. By utilizing on the web assets and learning stages successfully, we can set out on an excursion of persistent development and expert improvement that engages us to flourish in the consistently impacting universe of remote work.

Making a Customized Learning Plan for Proficient Development

In the huge spread of persistent learning and expert turn of events, a customized learning plan arises as a reference point of direction, enlightening the way to development and progression in the remote work scene. This part digs into the complexities of making a custom-made learning plan, offering bits of knowledge and methodologies to assist telecommuters with putting forth objectives, distinguish learning open doors, and diagram a course towards their ideal expert objective.

Start by considering your vocation yearnings, assets, and regions for development to acquire clearness on your expert objectives and needs. Characterize explicit, quantifiable, and reachable targets that line up with your drawn out vision and goals, guaranteeing that they are sensible and feasible inside the setting of your ongoing job and conditions.

Recognize the abilities, information, and capabilities expected to accomplish your expert objectives, leading a complete abilities evaluation to pinpoint solid areas and regions for development. Utilize this data to focus on learning targets and spotlight your endeavors on obtaining the abilities and skills that are generally pertinent and valuable to your professional success.

Investigate a different scope of learning open doors and assets to help your expert development and improvement, including on the web courses, studios, meetings, and mentorship programs. Tailor your learning intend to oblige different learning styles and inclinations, integrating a blend of independent learning, intelligent studios, and experiential mastering potential chances to upgrade your abilities and information.

Lay out a timetable and achievements to keep tabs on your development towards accomplishing your learning objectives, setting cutoff times and designated spots to consider yourself responsible and remain focused. Separate bigger learning targets into more modest, sensible errands and dispense time and assets as needs be, guaranteeing that you gain reliable headway towards your expert advancement objectives.

As you leave on the excursion of persistent learning and expert development, let your customized learning plan be your compass, directing you towards your objective with clearness and reason. By defining clear objectives, recognizing learning open doors, and diagramming a course for your expert turn of events, you can open your maximum capacity and flourish in the remote work scene with certainty and conviction.

9

Chapter 9: Troubleshooting Common Remote Work Challenges

Recognizing Normal Remote Work Difficulties

As remote work keeps on multiplying, it carries with it a novel arrangement of difficulties that can block efficiency and thwart achievement. This part leaves on an exhaustive investigation of the normal obstacles experienced by telecommuters, revealing insight into their subtleties and suggestions in the computerized scene.

Remote work, while offering adaptability and independence, likewise presents deterrents that telecommuters should explore. From mechanical errors to correspondence boundaries and battles with balance between fun and serious activities, these difficulties can appear in different structures and effect various parts of remote work life.

One of the essential difficulties looked by telecommuters is the dependence on innovation, which can be inclined to errors and interruptions. Web network issues, programming similarity issues, and equipment breakdowns are normal events that can disturb work process and impede efficiency.

correspondence manners. Set assumptions around accessibility and responsiveness, guaranteeing that everybody is in total agreement and knows how to connect with associates when required.

Besides, cultivate a culture of straightforwardness and transparency inside your group, empowering ordinary correspondence and data sharing. Keep colleagues informed about project updates, achievements, and choices, and give open doors to them to get clarification on some pressing issues, share thoughts, and give input.

To improve cooperation in virtual groups, focus on collaboration and aggregate critical thinking. Empower joint effort on undertakings and assignments, utilizing the different abilities and viewpoints of colleagues to accomplish ideal outcomes. Utilize cooperative instruments and stages to work with meetings to generate new ideas, record sharing, and ongoing coordinated effort, permitting colleagues to cooperate successfully no matter what their actual area.

Finally, put resources into building trust and affinity among colleagues, as trust is the groundwork of compelling correspondence and joint effort in virtual groups. Cultivate a feeling of fellowship and common regard through group building exercises, get-togethers, and casual collaborations, permitting colleagues to manufacture significant associations and reinforce their bond collectively.

By executing these procedures and cultivating a culture of correspondence and cooperation inside your virtual group, you can conquer the obstructions of distance and accomplish striking outcomes together. Make sure to focus on lucidity, straightforwardness, and cooperation in your associations, and influence innovation to work with consistent correspondence and coordinated effort in the computerized work area.

Tending to Balance between fun and serious activities and Prosperity

Keeping a sound balance between fun and serious activities is fundamental for telecommuters to flourish both by and by and expertly. This part investigates procedures for accomplishing balance between work liabilities and individual prosperity, guaranteeing that telecommuters can lead satisfying lives while succeeding in their expert undertakings.

One of the vital systems for advancing balance between serious and fun activities is to lay out clear limits among work and individual life. Characterize explicit work hours and assign a devoted work area where you can zero in on work without interruptions. At the point when your normal business day closes, put forth a cognizant attempt to separate from business related errands and take part in exercises that revive and re-energize you.

Furthermore, focus on taking care of oneself and prosperity as fundamental parts of your everyday daily practice. Consolidate customary activity, care practices, and side interests into your timetable to support your physical, mental, and close to home wellbeing. Enjoy reprieves over the course of the day to rest and re-energize, permitting yourself an opportunity to de-pressurize and re-energize your batteries.

Set sensible assumptions for you and others in regards to responsibility and efficiency. Perceive that it's OK to express no to extra errands or solicitations that might infringe upon your own time. Discuss straightforwardly with your partners and administrators about your limits and constraints, pushing for your prosperity and looking for help when required.

Besides, embrace the adaptability that remote work bears to make a timetable that lines up with your singular inclinations and needs. Explore different avenues regarding various schedules and methodologies to find what turns out best for you, permitting you to figure out some kind of harmony among work and individual life.

At last, look for help from companions, family, and partners to explore the difficulties of remote work and keep a sound balance between serious and fun activities. Rest on your encouraging group of people for support, guidance, and point of view, knowing that you're in good company in your excursion to focus on prosperity and joy.

By executing these techniques and focusing on balance between fun and serious activities and prosperity, telecommuters can accomplish more noteworthy satisfaction and fulfillment in both their own and proficient lives. Recall that equilibrium appears to be unique for everybody, so be thoughtful to yourself and make changes on a case by case basis to guarantee that your work and individual life are as one.

10

Chapter 10: Sustaining Productivity and Success in the Long Run

Laying out Feasible Work Propensities

In the long distance race of remote work, supportability is critical to keeping up with efficiency and staying balanced over an extended time. This part dives into the craft of developing feasible work propensities, offering experiences and systems to lay out limits, oversee responsibility really, and sustain prosperity in the remote work scene.

Integral to supporting efficiency and achievement is the foundation of clear limits among work and individual life. Set explicit work hours and assign a devoted work area where you can zero in on errands without interruptions. At the point when your assigned work hours come to a nearby, deliberately change into individual time, detaching from business related liabilities to re-energize and revive.

Besides, focus on responsibility the executives to forestall overpower and keep a feasible speed of work. Separate errands into reasonable pieces, focus on undertakings in view of criticalness and significance, and set practical assumptions for what you can achieve inside a given

49

learning amazing open doors that line up with your inclinations, objectives, and yearnings.

Put forth substantial objectives for your expert development and advancement, laying out clear targets and achievements to direct your excursion. Recognize regions for development and development, and make a customized learning plan that frames explicit activities and moves toward accomplish your ideal results.

Additionally, look for input and mentorship from associates, companions, and industry specialists to speed up your learning and improvement. Embrace useful analysis as a significant instrument for development, and effectively search out chances to gain from others and grow your viewpoint.

By focusing on proficient development and advancement, telecommuters can future-evidence their professions and stay serious in the consistently changing scene of remote work. Recall that putting resources into yourself is the best venture you can make, and that the excursion of expert development is however compensating as it seems to be advancing. With devotion, steadiness, and a pledge to deep rooted learning, you can support long haul achievement and satisfaction in the remote work scene.

Cultivating Significant Associations and Local area

In the midst of the computerized spread of remote work, encouraging significant associations and developing a feeling of local area arises as fundamental elements for supporting inspiration, commitment, and accomplishment long term. This part investigates the significance of building compatibility, teaming up successfully, and supporting a feeling of having a place in virtual workplaces, offering techniques and practices to cultivate association and local area among telecommuters.

Perceive the innate worth of human association in the remote work scene, recognizing that social bonds and connections are imperative for keeping up with confidence, inspiration, and prosperity. Put forth a cognizant attempt to focus on relational associations, contacting partners for virtual espresso visits, casual registrations, or virtual group building exercises to encourage kinship and construct compatibility.

Set out open doors for cooperation and collaboration inside your virtual group, utilizing computerized stages and instruments to work with significant communications and joint ventures. Empower open correspondence, thought sharing, and joint effort on errands and drives, permitting colleagues to use their aggregate assets and aptitude to accomplish shared objectives and targets.

Besides, put resources into building a feeling of local area inside your remote group, encouraging a steady and comprehensive climate where everybody feels esteemed, regarded, and heard. Praise accomplishments, achievements, and triumphs together, and offer help and consolation to partners during testing times.

Draw in with more extensive expert networks and organizations to extend your associations and access significant assets, bits of knowledge, and valuable open doors. Partake in industry discussions, virtual systems administration occasions, and online networks to associate with similar people, share encounters, and trade thoughts.

By encouraging significant associations and local area in the remote work scene, telecommuters can battle sensations of segregation, improve coordinated effort and collaboration, and develop a feeling of having a place that supports inspiration and commitment over the long haul. Recollect that we are more grounded together, and that by supporting connections and building local area, we can flourish in the advanced domain of remote work with flexibility, reason, and satisfaction.

Conclusion:

Considering the Remote Work Excursion

As we come to the finish of this excursion through the complexities of remote work, it's basic to stop and consider the way we've navigated. Pause for a minute to think back on your own remote work venture, recognizing the achievements you've reached, the difficulties you've survived, and the development you've encountered en route.

Reflection fills in as a useful asset for mindfulness and contemplation, empowering us to acquire important experiences into our assets, shortcomings, and regions for development in the remote work scene. Consider the illustrations you've mastered and the abilities you've sharpened all through your remote work insight, perceiving the worth of each victory and difficulty in forming your expert process.

Additionally, utilize this chance for reflection to praise your accomplishments and achievements in remote work, regardless of how enormous or little. Whether it's dominating another expertise, defeating a difficult venture, or cultivating significant associations with partners, invest heavily in your triumphs and recognize the commitment and exertion you've put resources into your remote work attempts.

As you think about your remote work venture, consider the examples you've advanced and how you can apply them to keep developing and advancing from here on out. Recognize regions where you can improve and define objectives for your continuous turn of events, focusing on an excursion of nonstop improvement and development in the remote work scene.

At last, reflection fills in as a compass directing us forward, enlightening the way forward with lucidity and reason. By finding opportunity to ponder your remote work venture, you can acquire important bits of knowledge, praise your accomplishments, and graph a course for future achievement and satisfaction in the computerized domain of remote work.

Embracing the Open doors Ahead

As we bid goodbye to this investigation of remote work, let us embrace the open doors that lie ahead with positive thinking and excitement. The excursion we've set out upon has revealed a scene rich with potential for development, development, and progress in the computerized domain. Now is the ideal time to throw away any waiting questions or reservations and embrace the future with great enthusiasm.

In the consistently developing scene of remote work, open doors flourish for the people who will hold onto them. From extending your range of abilities and investigating new vocation ways to utilizing innovation to upgrade efficiency and cooperation, the potential outcomes are inestimable. Embrace change as an impetus for development and change, perceiving that each new test presents a chance to learn, adjust, and flourish.

Besides, move toward the future with flexibility, versatility, and a development outlook. As telecommuters, we should be ready to explore the exciting bends in the road of the computerized scene with elegance and assurance. Embrace mishaps as any open doors for development, misfortunes as any open doors for learning, and change as any open doors for advancement. With flexibility as your safeguard and versatility as your compass, you can explore the vulnerabilities of remote work with certainty and balance.

Most importantly, keep a feeling of interest and miracle as you set out on this next part of your remote work venture. Embrace each new open door with energy and a receptive outlook, realizing that the best experiences are many times tracked down in the unfamiliar regions of the unexplored world. By embracing the potential open doors that lie ahead with positive thinking and energy, you can outline a course for progress and satisfaction in the steadily changing scene of remote work.

Focusing on Deep rooted Learning and Development

As we finish up our investigation of remote work, let us reaffirm our obligation to long lasting learning and self-improvement. In the our remote workplaces, knowing that together, we can make a strong, comprehensive, and flourishing computerized work environment where everybody feels esteemed, upheld, and engaged to accomplish their maximum capacity. By focusing on connections, joint effort, and encouraging groups of people, we can produce a way towards progress and satisfaction in the consistently developing scene of remote work.

www.ingramcontent.com/pod-product-compliance
Lightning Source LLC
Chambersburg PA
CBHW032002140726
47988CB00019B/3142